EXPLORING ARTIFICIAL INTELLIGENCE

THE FUTURE OF AI

Lisa Idzikowski

Lerner Publications ◆ Minneapolis

For my family

Lerner Publications Company
An imprint of Lerner Publishing Group, Inc.
241 First Avenue North
Minneapolis, MN 55401 USA

For reading levels and more information, look up this title at www.lernerbooks.com.

Main body text set in Aptifer Sans LT Pro.
Typeface provided by Linotype AG.

Editor: Nicole Berglund **Photo Editor:** Nicole Berglund
Lerner team: Martha Kranes

Library of Congress Cataloging-in-Publication Data

Names: Idzikowski, Lisa, author.
Title: The future of AI / Lisa Idzikowski.
Description: Minneapolis : Lerner Publications, [2025] | Series: Exploring Artificial Intelligence | Includes bibliographical references and index. | Audience: Ages 8–12 | Audience: Grades 4–6 | Summary: "What will AI look like in the future? Readers explore the history of AI and analyze where this technology might be headed"— Provided by publisher.
Identifiers: LCCN 2024017102 (print) | LCCN 2024017103 (ebook) | ISBN 9798765647905 (lib. bdg.) | ISBN 9798765661673 (pbk) | ISBN 9798765654552 (epub)
Subjects: LCSH: Artificial intelligence—Juvenile literature.
Classification: LCC Q335.4 .I39 2025 (print) | LCC Q335.4 (ebook) | DDC 006.3—dc23/eng/20240628

LC record available at https://lccn.loc.gov/2024017102
LC ebook record available at https://lccn.loc.gov/2024017103

Manufactured in the United States of America
1-1011015-53351-8/6/2024

TABLE OF CONTENTS

INTRODUCTION
Look Closely 4

CHAPTER 1
From Turing to Today 7

CHAPTER 2
Roadblocks to Future AI 15

CHAPTER 3
Be Bold 20

CHAPTER 4
Friend or Foe? 27

Glossary 30

Learn More 31

Index 32

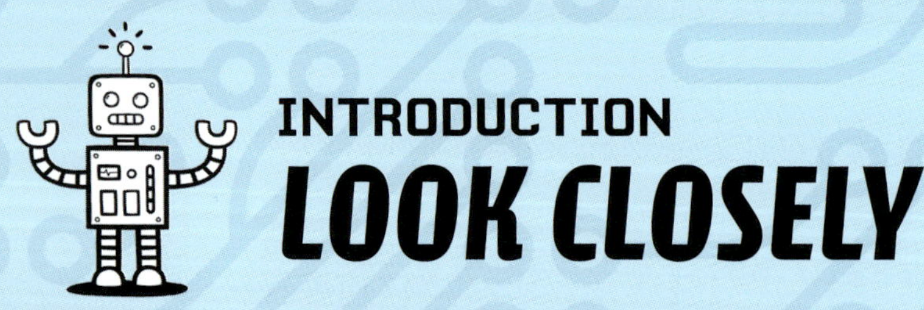

INTRODUCTION

LOOK CLOSELY

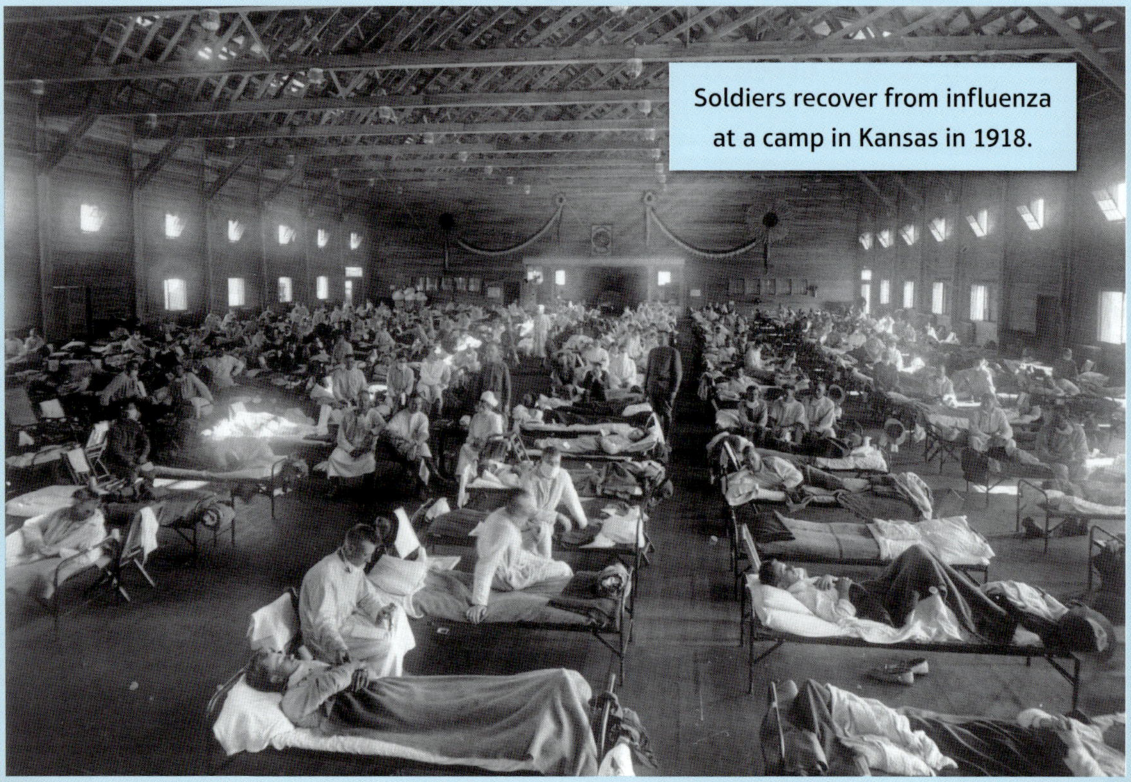

Soldiers recover from influenza at a camp in Kansas in 1918.

The world has suffered two deadly illnesses in just over one hundred years. An outbreak of influenza, or the flu, began in 1918 during World War I (1914–1918). It likely started in the United States, then spread worldwide. More than one hundred years later, in 2019, the world faced a new challenge, COVID-19. COVID-19 may have begun in China, but like the flu, it spread around the world quickly. Each pandemic lasted over two years, and millions of people died.

Many things were similar about these two outbreaks. But there was one big difference between them. In 1918 no vaccines protecting against the flu existed. It took almost thirty years before a flu vaccine was made.

The first COVID-19 vaccines were released in December 2020, less than one year from the start of the pandemic.

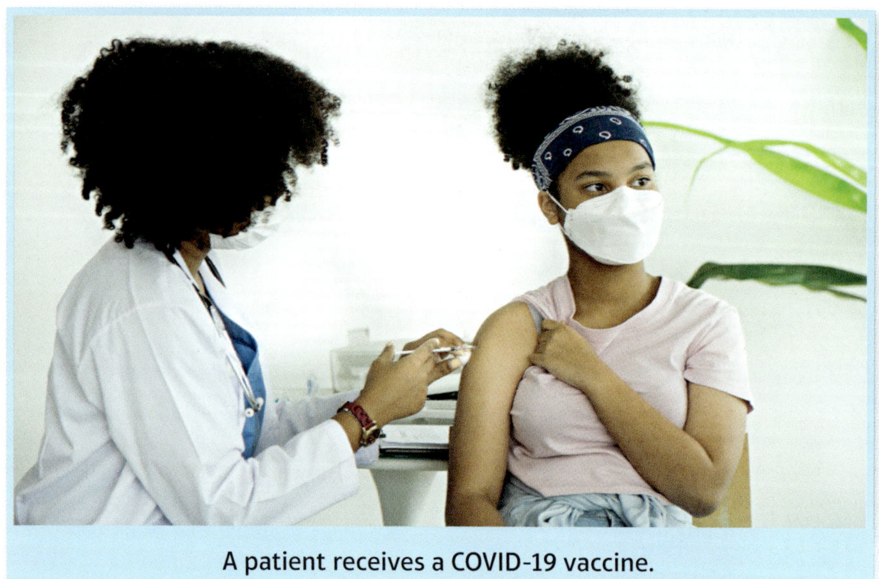
A patient receives a COVID-19 vaccine.

Artificial intelligence (AI) detected COVID-19 before it spread worldwide. This information was important because it could help politicians make policies to prevent COVID-19 from spreading. It could also help doctors treat patients and create a vaccine. During the outbreak, deep learning systems identified old and new drugs to use as treatments. These drugs aided researchers who were developing vaccines. AI also made it possible to diagnose infected people and help them receive treatment quickly. AI helped researchers create a vaccine in record time, but AI technology was being developed long before the COVID-19 pandemic.

A woman makes a call using a landline phone.

CHAPTER 1

FROM TURING TO TODAY

In 1950 people did not carry cell phones. They had to call people from landlines. No one had computers at home either. Families watched black-and-white TV and listened to music on the radio. There was no internet, no video games, and no AI.

Alan Turing (*inset*) invented a machine to decode secret messages. Turing's Bombe device (*above*) was used during World War II (1939–1945).

Though technology at this time was not as advanced as today, people were working on early computers and AI. A British mathematician named Alan Turing wondered if machines could think. He also designed machines including the Automatic Computing Engine, a digital computer that could store programs.

Turing's impact sparked many advancements in his field. The term *artificial intelligence* was first used by John McCarthy in 1955. McCarthy wrote LISP, the first computer language used in AI, a few years later. Then researchers made machines modeled after human brain cells. Arthur Samuel built a computer program to play checkers in 1962. Then in 1966 Joseph Weizenbaum created Eliza, an early AI program. Eliza's system acted as a therapist and answered people's questions or gave advice. Soon after Eliza, one of the first moving robots, Shakey, came out. Shakey's AI software let it move from room to room and interact with moving objects.

John McCarthy created LISP in the late 1950s and wrote a paper about the computer language in 1960.

Experts Have It

The next stage of AI came when computer scientists used knowledge from experts to make machines act smart. Engineers gathered facts and information from an expert. Then they programmed this knowledge into machines.

Edward Feigenbaum helped create DENDRAL.

DENDRAL, created in 1965, was one such expert system. The system assisted chemists with analyzing chemical compounds. DENDRAL is an example of how an AI system does one task very well. This is called an artificial narrow intelligence.

Garry Kasparov (*left*) plays chess against Deep Blue, controlled by scientist Murray Campbell.

Better and Better

Advances in computer science continued. In 1997 a chess-playing computer program, Deep Blue, and world chess champion Garry Kasparov played each other in a match. The two had already competed the previous year, when Kasparov won. This time, many were surprised when Deep Blue won the game. Deep Blue was programmed to understand chess. But engineers didn't stop there.

They wanted to make their game systems and other machines smarter. They used an AI technology called machine learning to do this.

Machine learning is a form of AI that has been around for more than seventy years. It uses data and algorithms to learn through experience. It sometimes needs humans to fix its errors. This tech controls many modern devices and systems. Machines such as Apple's Siri or Amazon's Alexa can understand spoken human languages. Systems such as Netflix or YouTube can suggest shows or videos similar to what you already enjoyed.

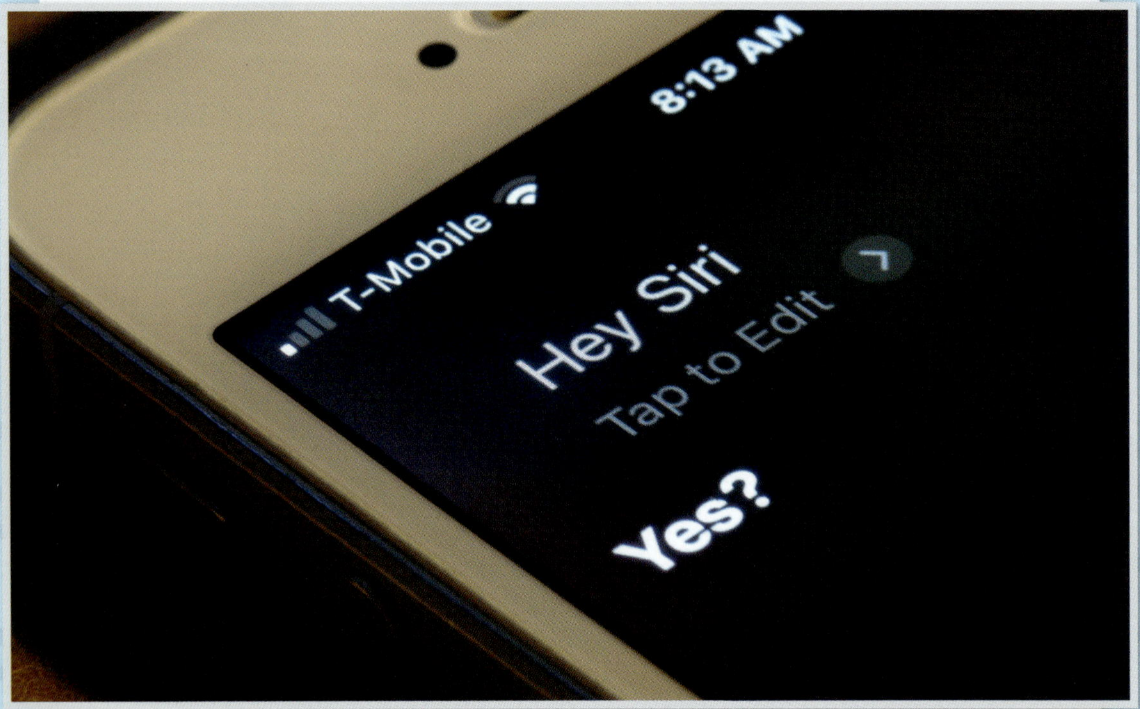

The app musical.ly was released in 2014, and in 2018 it merged with another app to become TikTok.

Deep learning is a more advanced technology than machine learning. Deep learning needs less help from humans and is modeled after the human brain. It powers self-driving cars and the social media platform TikTok.

The next wave of smart systems seems poised to create things. Generative AI models produce text, images, music, and more. With generative AI, programmers can write code faster and train chatbots. Scientists might even discover new molecules with generative AI!

To the Future and Beyond

What will the future look like for AI? That's not easy to say. Right now, AIs have artificial narrow intelligence. This means that they can do specific tasks well. AI soccer robots, for example, are trained to play soccer. They play the game well, but they couldn't drive a car or write a shopping list. The goal of some computer scientists is to invent artificial general intelligence (AGI). AGI machines would think, act, and do multiple tasks in many settings, just as people do.

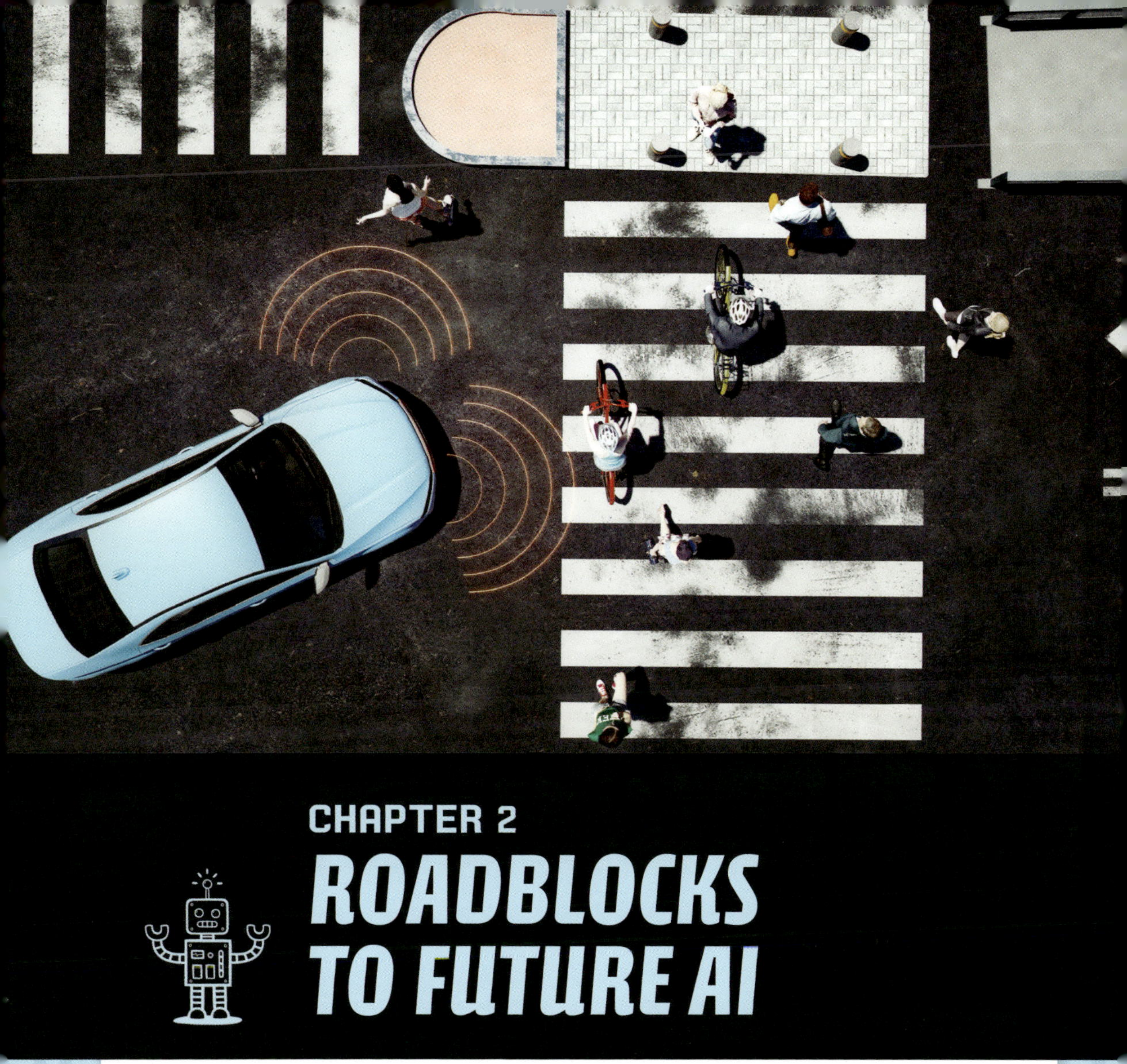

CHAPTER 2

ROADBLOCKS TO FUTURE AI

AI is useful in many ways. It unlocks smartphones after recognizing a person's face. It allows self-driving cars to spot moving objects. In power plants, it directs electrical power to the places that need it most. Engineers are building AI systems that will do more and more. But are there roadblocks in the way for advancing AI?

Computer servers are more powerful than laptop or desktop computers.

Too Much Energy

Every day data centers full of computer servers gobble up electricity. The same amount of energy used in one day at a ChatGPT data center could power over thirty thousand homes. These data centers also need to stay cool. Large amounts of water are used to keep temperatures down. Using all this water and electricity can be expensive to maintain, and it harms the environment.

Without question, AI will improve. Artificial general intelligence might be coming next. More and more energy will be needed to keep these powerful systems running. Where will it come from? Scientists and engineers are working on this problem. Some suggest making algorithms that work with less electricity. Others insist that more energy must come from nuclear power.

Algorithms are sets of instructions used by computers to complete tasks.

Nuclear Power

Nuclear power provides energy. In nuclear power plants today, energy is produced when atoms split into two or more parts. Experts say that AI systems of the future will need much more power to run. They say another energy type must be developed. This kind of energy would be produced when two atoms join together.

Pharmacists hand out medicine prescribed by doctors. Some people question whether AI could handle this complex job.

Lack of Trust

The use of AI systems is everywhere, from our smartphones to our cars. This technology is being used more and more every day. But many people do not trust AI. Many Americans think people would do a better job than AI at making laws, handing out medicine, or teaching. Experts say that without trust, people will avoid using AI. This will harm the future of this technology.

CHAPTER 3

BE BOLD

Throughout time, humans have invented bold technologies. Airplanes, vaccines, and the internet are among these. AI might be the boldest invention yet. Will it find life on another planet? Will AI find new cures for diseases? There is much that we do not know, but one thing is certain. The future of AI will be exciting.

Way Out There

Is life beyond Earth possible or just a dream of science fiction? Scientists at NASA are searching for signs of life beyond Earth. They have a target. They want to travel to Europa, one of Jupiter's moons. Advanced AI is needed for missions like this.

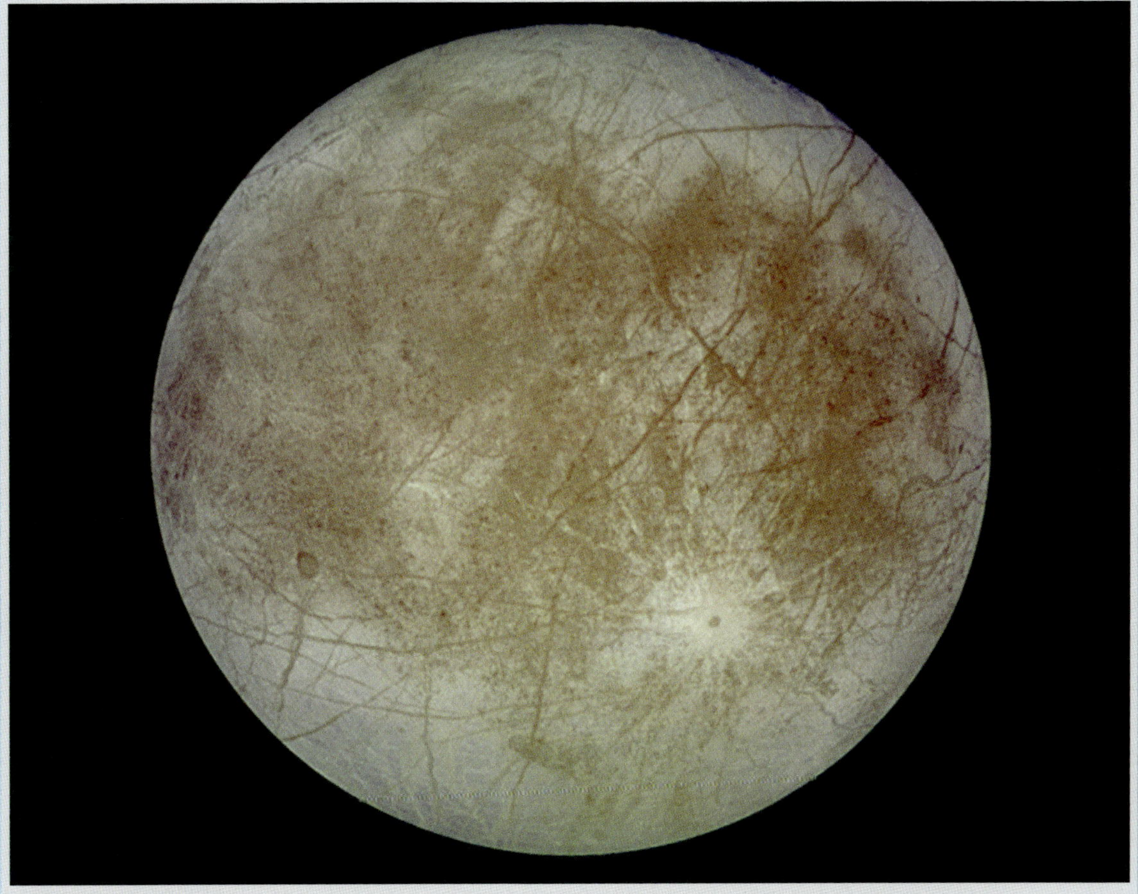

Europa is one of Jupiter's largest moons.

Scientists believe there is a large ocean under Europa's icy surface. On a future mission, a spacecraft would travel there, land, and melt through the ice. Melting might take a whole Earth year. The spacecraft would lower a special machine into the water. It would swim around and collect data. The AI on board would search for areas of heat that may show signs of life on this moon.

This model shows the ocean that may be beneath Europa's surface.

STEVE CHIEN

Steve Chien is a senior research scientist at NASA. He leads NASA's AI group at the Jet Propulsion Laboratory in California. Chien wants to use spacecraft to observe the farthest reaches of space and find alien life. To do this, space probes and rovers must have incredible AI. Chien's team works to invent these AI systems.

NASA's Jet Propulsion Laboratory

AI in Disguise

NASA scientists wonder if one of Saturn's moons has life. Icy Enceladus (*below*) has a saltwater ocean that may support life, just like Earth's oceans. The Exobiology Extant Life Surveyor (EELS) is a snake-like AI robot. It was created to explore the watery world of Enceladus. The 14-foot (4.3 m) EELS has sensors and cameras for observation. EELS isn't ready to explore the far worlds of space yet, but one day it will be.

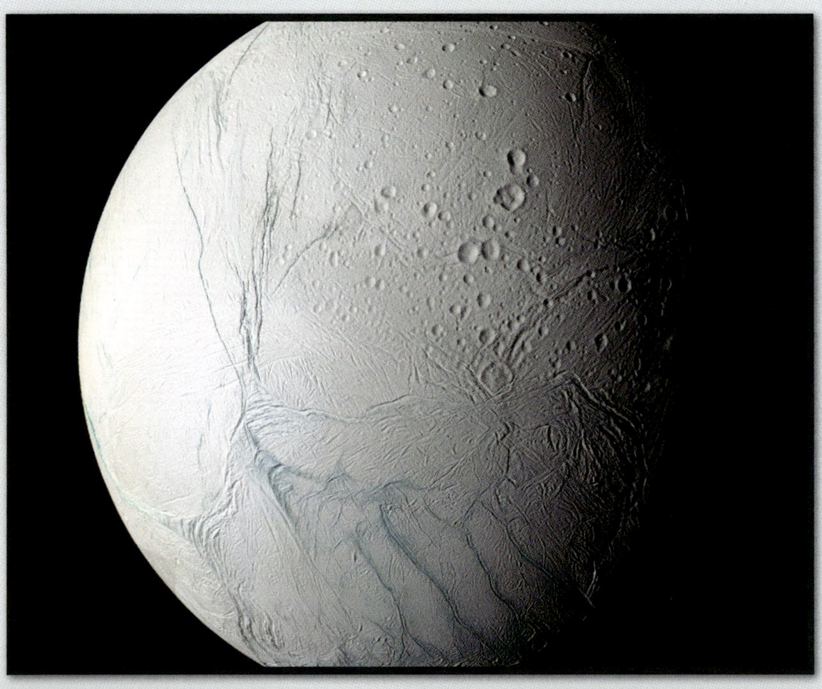

Inside the Body

Here on Earth, AI is already making a difference in medicine. Doctors use AI to help treat cancer and read X-rays. AI-powered robots aid doctors during surgeries. AI is also helping discover new medicines. Superbug infections are caused by bacteria that resist normal medicine. New AI-produced drugs might be able to kill these bacteria and cure the infection.

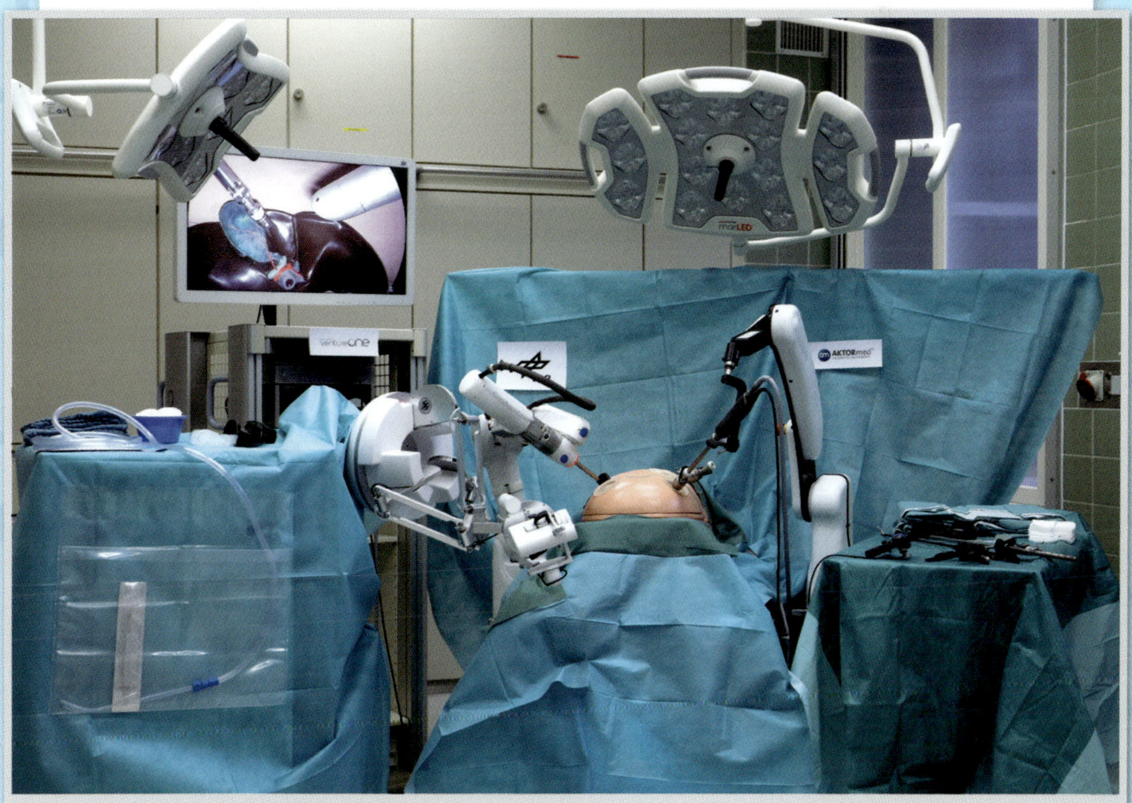

The ForNeRo research network created this AI-powered surgery robot.

A woman wears a brain-computer interface device to control a computer with her mind.

Some people have lost movement in their arms or legs. Could AI technology help? Researchers are experimenting with brain-computer interface (BCI) to help paralyzed individuals. With BCI, a paralyzed person might operate an artificial limb just by thinking about it. In 2024 a BCI chip was placed into a person's brain. This person recovered well and could control a computer mouse just by thinking!

CHAPTER 4

FRIEND OR FOE?

Scientists, engineers, AI experts, and others think AI will affect the world in multiple ways. Many believe AI's influence will be positive. Students will have their own AI tutors for learning. People will sit back while their self-driving cars take them from place to place. Advances in medicine, including in surgery and vaccine science, will happen. But AI tools come with risks.

What If?

Tech experts have many concerns about the future of AI. People might use AI to create chaos with cyberattacks. Some experts' biggest fear is that false facts will spread online and create confusion. This could affect voters and elections. Jobs may be lost too. AI has already replaced some jobs formerly performed by factory and fast-food workers.

In 2023 the UK hosted the first AI Safety Summit, and it's become a yearly event.

Lots of Hope

Yet there is much hope for the future. AI experts are working to keep the world safe from AI misuse. In May 2023, more than three hundred researchers, engineers, and executives signed an online statement from the Center for AI Safety urging a worldwide effort to protect against the risks of AI. The signers agreed that the world must work together to be safe with AI. Experts cannot totally predict the future of AI or the roles that AI will play in our lives. But AI is already at work every day. With safety rules and protections in place, AI can be put to good use.

Glossary

artificial general intelligence (AGI): artificial intelligence that nears the level of human intelligence

artificial intelligence (AI): technology that gives computers and machines humanlike intelligence

atom: the smallest particle in existence

brain-computer interface (BCI): a communication system that allows people to control machines by using their thoughts

computer server: a type of large computer that offers services to the smaller computers connected to it

cyberattack: an attack on a computer system that is meant to cause harm

deep learning: the way a machine learns without human help

generative AI: a type of artificial intelligence that produces something new such as text, images, videos, or music

machine learning: the way a machine learns from algorithms and data, though it sometimes needs humans to fix its errors

Learn More

Britannica Kids: COVID-19
https://kids.britannica.com/students/article/COVID-19/634816

Britannica Kids: Jupiter
https://kids.britannica.com/students/article/Jupiter/345009

Idzikowski, Lisa. *The Challenges of AI*. Minneapolis: Lerner Publications, 2025.

Mattern, Joanne. *All About Artificial Intelligence*. Lake Elmo, MN: Focus Readers, 2023.

National Geographic Kids: Passport to Space
https://kids.nationalgeographic.com/space

Olson, Elsie. *AI Safety*. Minneapolis: Lerner Publications, 2025.

Science Kids: The History of Robotics
https://www.sciencekids.co.nz/sciencefacts/technology/historyofrobotics.html

Thorpe, Judy. *What's Artificial Intelligence?* Buffalo: KidHaven, 2025.

Index

brain-computer interface (BCI), 26

Center for AI Safety, 29
Chien, Steve, 23
COVID-19, 5–6

Deep Blue, 11
DENDRAL, 10

Eliza, 9
Enceladus, 24
Europa, 21–22
Exobiology Extant Life Surveyor (EELS), 24

generative AI, 13

influenza, 4–5

LISP, 8

McCarthy, John, 8

NASA, 21, 23–24
nuclear power, 17–18

Samuel, Arthur, 9
Shakey, 9

Turing, Alan, 8

vaccine, 5–6, 20, 27

Weizenbaum, Joseph, 9

Photo Acknowledgments

Image credits: GL Archive/Alamy, p. 4; Xinhua News Agency/Getty Images, p. 5; Kriangkrai Thitimakorn/Getty Images, p. 6; Three Lions/Stringer/Getty Images, p. 7; Science History Images/Alamy, pp. 8 (left), 21; Wikimedia Commons PD, p. 8 (right); Roger Ressmeyer/Getty Images, p. 9; US Air Force/Wikimedia Commons PD, p. 10; STAN HONDA/Stringer/Getty Images, p. 11; Ted Hsu/Alamy, p. 12; Kaspars Grinvalds/Shutterstock, p. 13; peterhowell/Getty Images, p. 14; gremlin/Getty Images, p. 15; Jason marz/Getty Images, p. 16; GCShutter/Getty Images, p. 17; aerial-photos.com/Alamy, p. 18; izusek/Getty Images, p. 19; Craig Hastings/Getty Images, p. 20; Mario Tama/Getty Images, p. 22; Christian Offenberg/Alamy, p. 23; AP Photo/NASA, p. 24; picture alliance/Getty Images, p. 25; AP Photo/John Locher, p. 26; FatCamera/Getty Images, p. 27; SolStock/Getty Images, p. 28; AP Photo/Leon Neal/EMPPL PA Wire, p. 29. Design elements: filo/Getty Images; JakeOlimb/Getty Images. Cover: CSA Images/Getty Images.